P9-CBI-916

ROBO-MOTION
ROBOTS THAT MOVE LIKE ANIMALS

Linda Zajac

Millbrook Press / Minneapolis

In memory of my mom, who had a big heart, bright smile, and lively gait —LZ

I'm grateful to the Connecticut Office of the Arts for their generous support. Special thanks to Dr. Andrew Biewener, professor of biology at Harvard University, for reviewing the manuscript. Many thanks to writing mavens Daryl and Natasha for their helpful advice and heartwarming words of encouragement. Thanks also to Carol, Allison, and the rest of the book-building team at Lerner for their eye-catching designs and collective expertise.

Millbrook Press™
An imprint of Lerner Publishing Group, Inc.
241 First Avenue North
Minneapolis, MN 55401 USA

For reading levels and more information, look up this title at www.lernerbooks.com.

Designed by Viet Chu.
Main body text set in Cineplex LT Pro.
Typeface provided by Linotype

Library of Congress Cataloging-in-Publication Data

Names: Zajac, Linda, 1960- author.
Title: Robo-motion : robots that move like animals / Linda Zajac.
Description: Minneapolis : Millbrook Press, 2022. | Includes bibliographical references. | Audience: Ages 4–9 | Audience: Grades 2–3 | Summary: "It's a bird, it's a plane, it's a . . . robot hummingbird? Meet robots inspired by animals that are racing through water like sharks, climbing walls like geckos, flying through the sky like honeybees, and more." — Provided by publisher.
Identifiers: LCCN 2019046396 (print) | LCCN 2019046397 (ebook) | ISBN 9781541581265 (library binding) | ISBN 9781728401546 (ebook)
Subjects: LCSH: Robots—Juvenile literature. | Robots—Motion—Juvenile literature.
Classification: LCC TJ211.2 .Z35 2022 (print) | LCC TJ211.2 (ebook) | DDC 629.8/932—dc23

LC record available at https://lccn.loc.gov/2019046396
LC ebook record available at https://lccn.loc.gov/2019046397

Manufactured in the United States of America
1-47325-47952-2/22/2021

Animals are motion masters. They skitter, scuttle, grip, glide, spring, cling, and more.

By building robots that mimic animal motion, we too can move like animals. With robo-motion, we can . . .

STRETCH like an octopus,
CURLING graceful limbs.

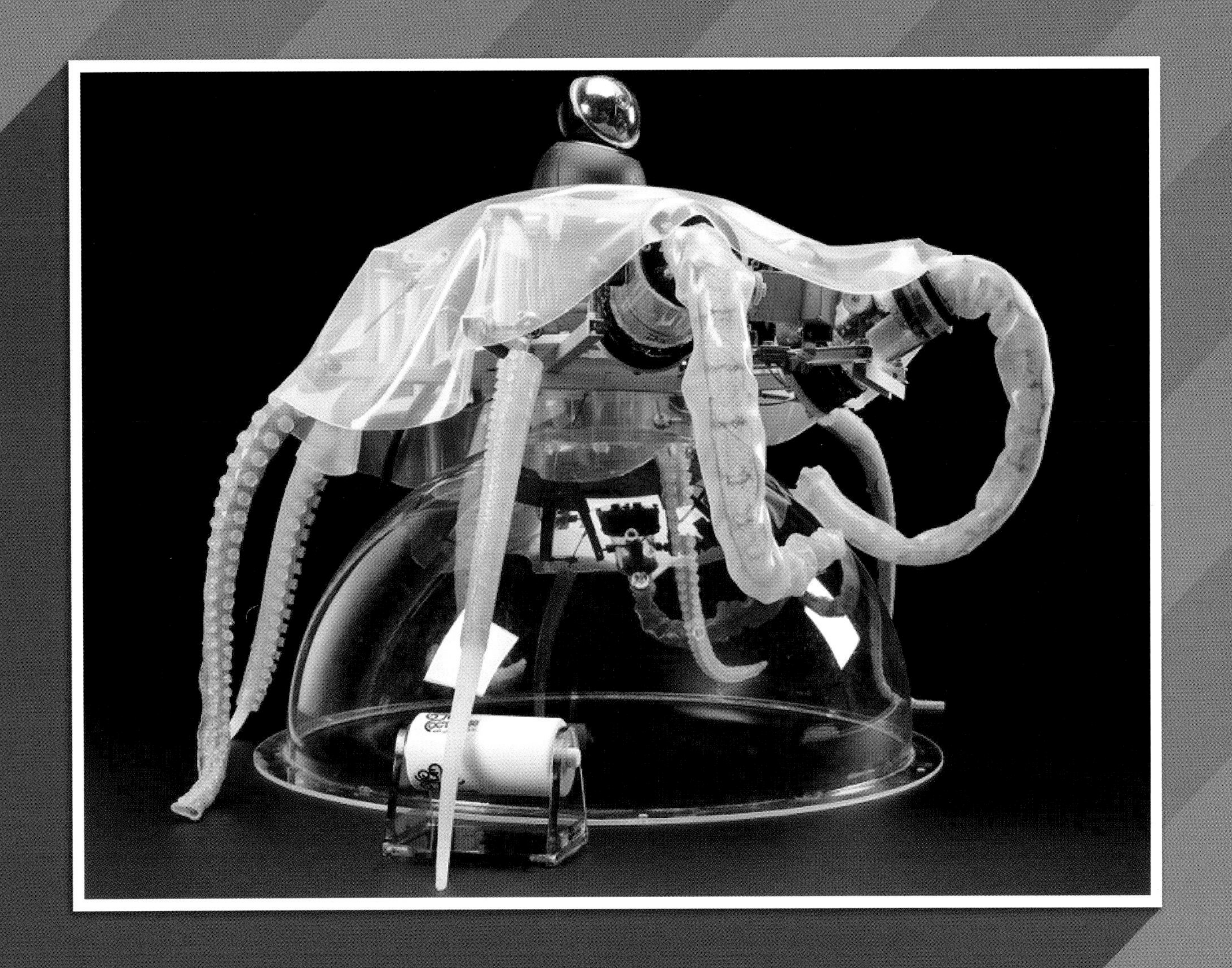

The OCTOPUS robot's soft arms gently curl and grip, so they could be helpful to doctors. Rubbery tools can bend around organs and reach into tight spaces during surgery.

CHASE like a cheetah,
CHARGING through the grass.

The MIT Cheetah robots run and jump over objects. And soon they'll be able to inspect disaster sites so that humans won't have to risk their lives.

SKITTER like a roach,
CREEPING into cracks.

Tough cockroaches scurry and squeeze their bodies through tiny openings. CRAM cockroach robots could help after an earthquake or other disaster by searching for survivors buried in tight spaces.

HOVER like a hummingbird,
FLYING overhead.

The Nano Air Vehicle (NAV) is a small robot that hovers like a hummingbird. As it travels on fast-beating wings, it can record live video. It was designed for spy missions in cities.

SCUTTLE like a crab,
SPLASHING through the surf.

Crabster CR200 is an underwater robot that's the size of a small car. Like a crab, it's sturdy and stable as it crawls through pounding surf and pulling tides. Crabster was made to explore the seafloor, respond to oil spills, search for shipwrecks, and check underwater pipelines.

BUZZ like a bee,
CRUISING with the swarm.

Scientists at the Wyss Institute at Harvard University are creating tiny RoboBees. One day they could be powered by the sun to fly on their own or work together as a swarm. These small microrobots could be used to monitor the weather or check on crops.

LURK like a shark,
SLICING through the sea.

GhostSwimmer mimics some of the fastest fish in the ocean. This robot, created for the US Navy, scans ship hulls, spies on enemies, and reports on tides, currents, and weather.

SPRING like a kangaroo,
BOUNCING off back legs.

When the BionicKangaroo leaps, it leans forward, flexing the rubbery springs in its legs. Energy from one jump powers the next jump. In factories where cars and other items are assembled, machines that operate the same way as this robot's legs may save space, money, and energy.

GRIP like a gecko,
CLINGING as it climbs.

StickyBot has tiny rubbery wedges beneath its toes similar to the tiny hairlike structures on a gecko's foot. They grip so that StickyBot can climb smooth surfaces. Robots like this one could repair spacecraft, check skyscrapers, and help with search and rescue missions.

SWOOP like a bat,
FLAPPING webbed wings.

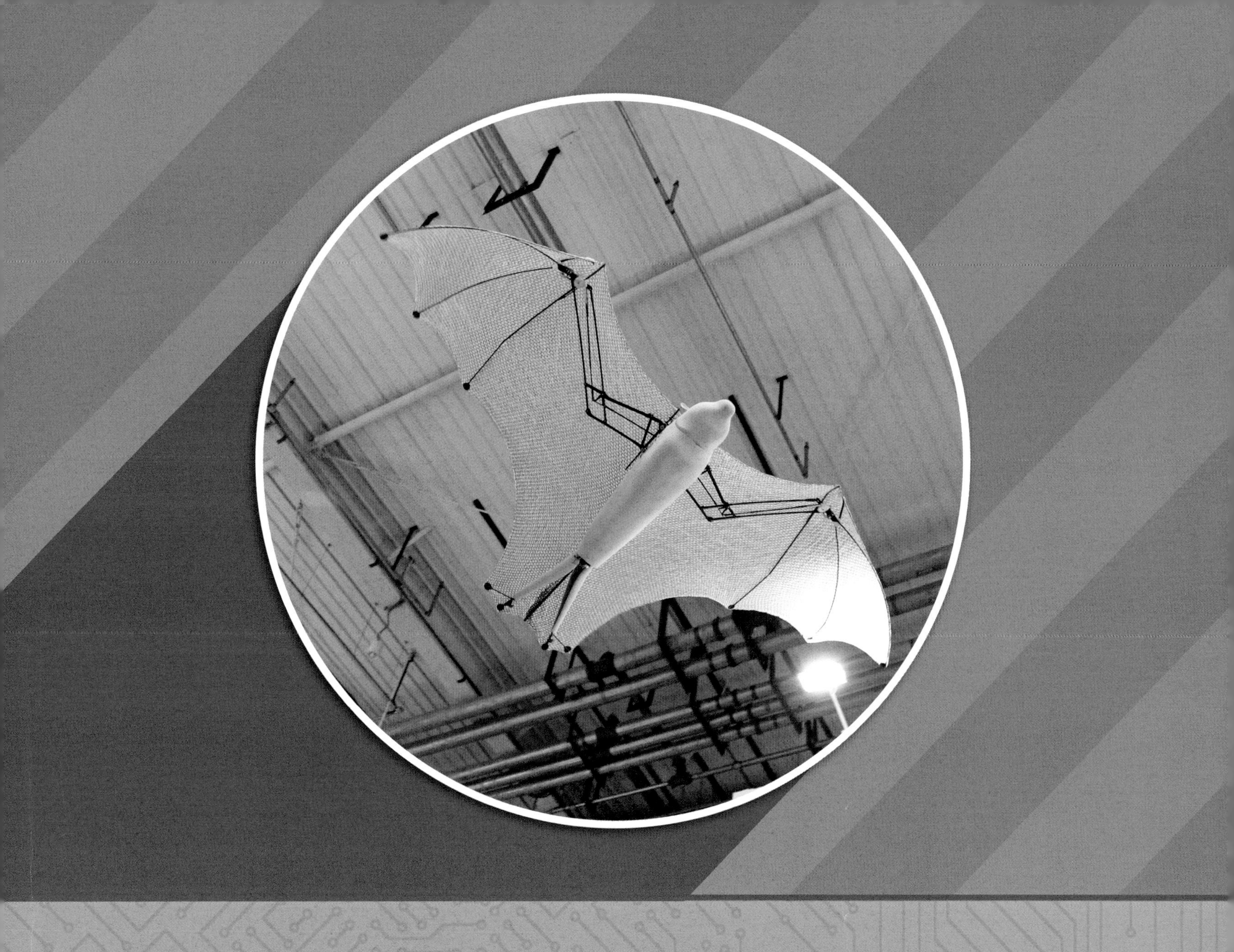

With gears and motors inside a foam body, BionicFlyingFox flies much like a flying fox bat. This drone's flexible wings flap and bend so that it can dart and turn in midair. The BionicFlyingFox is a model for other drones because it can fly even when its ultralight elastic wings are damaged.

GLIDE like a jellyfish,

RIDING on the tide.

AquaJellies are soft-bodied robots that swim like jellyfish. Sensors in the robots track their positions as they measure water temperature and the current. With a smartphone that controls Aquajellies, water plant workers could use them to monitor water conditions and detect problems faster.

HUSTLE like a hero,
RUSHING to the rescue.

Atlas jumps, lifts, flips, and stands up after a fall just as a human would. This heavy-duty humanoid could become a first responder for wildfires, oil spills, nuclear disasters, and other dangers.

Animals move in all kinds of amazing ways. And with engineering skills and some trial and error, we can build robots that skitter, scuttle, grip, glide, spring, cling, and more!

What else can we do with robo-motion? Take a close look at the animals all around you—the next discovery could be yours!

BLUEPRINTS FROM NATURE

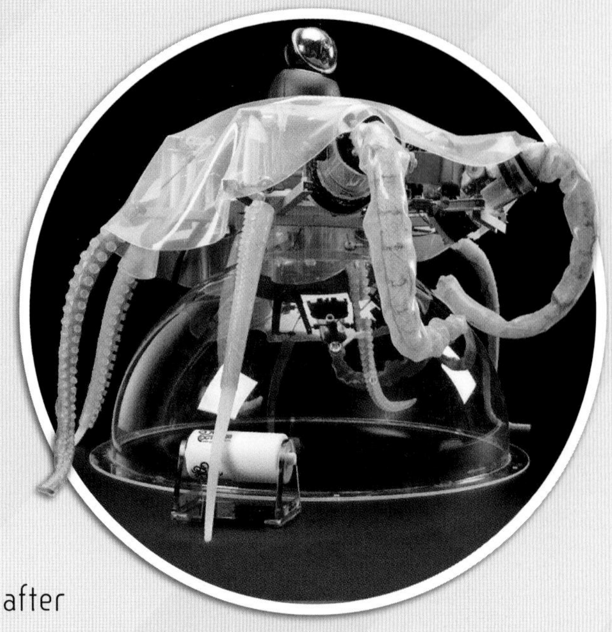

In fields and forests, on peaks and plains, nature can inspire scientists. That's because plants and animals have remarkable ways of doing things. Designs found in the natural world can work as blueprints or models to copy. ***Biomimicry*** is the term for human-made designs that imitate those found in nature.

By closely studying plants and animals, scientists have created a variety of new products and materials. An engineer invented Velcro after plucking cocklebur seeds from his dog's fur. Japanese engineers shaped the nose of a bullet train like the beak of a bird called a kingfisher, which made the train faster and quieter when traveling through tunnels. Scientists have created new materials based on studies of spider silk, sharkskin, mantis shrimp shells, and even slug slime.

Why is nature such a good model? Plants and animals have had thousands—or sometimes even millions—of years to evolve. Through this gradual process of change, species with traits that help them survive live longer lives and pass on those helpful traits to their young. And the species in that next generation with the most helpful traits again live longer and pass on those traits to their young. Little by little, plants and animals change in ways that help them flourish in their environments.

With robo-motion and biomimicry, we can learn from nature to improve the way we work and expand what we can do. We can save energy, money, time, and lives. While robots may seem anything but natural, the most effective robots may just be those inspired by nature!

GLOSSARY

biomimicry: copying nature to solve problems and advance science

blueprint: plan, model, or design

current: flow of water in a certain direction

design: plans used to make something

hull: main body of a ship

humanoid: a nonhuman creature that looks or acts like a human

microbots: tiny robots

mimic: copy

sensor: a device that reacts to changes in something such as light, heat, sound, or movement

stable: not easily tipped or pushed

tide: the regular rising and falling of the ocean

FURTHER READING

Ansberry, Karen. *Nature Did It First: Engineering through Biomimicry*. Nevada City, CA: Dawn, 2020.

Becker, Helaine. *Hubots: Real-World Robots Inspired by Humans*. Toronto: Kids Can, 2018.

DePrisco, Dorothea. *Animals on the Move*. New York: Liberty Street, 2017.

Jenkins, Steve. *Flying Frogs and Walking Fish: Leaping Lemurs, Tumbling Toads, Jet-Propelled Jellyfish, and More Surprising Ways That Animals Move*. Boston: Houghton Mifflin Harcourt, 2016.

Nordstrom, Kristen. *Mimic Makers: Biomimicry Inventors Inspired by Nature*. Watertown, MA: Charlesbridge, 2021.

Schaefer, Lola. *Flying Robots*. Minneapolis: Lerner Publications, 2021.

Simons, Lisa. *Beastly Robots: Military Technology Inspired by Animals*. North Mankato: Capstone. 2020.

Watson, Galadriel. *Running Wild: Awesome Animals in Motion*. Toronto: Annick, 2020.

PHOTO ACKNOWLEDGMENTS

Image credits: kuritafsheen/Getty Images, pp. 2-3; Henner Damke/Shutterstock.com, p. 4; © Jennie Hills, pp. 5, 30; Stu Porter/Shutterstock.com, p. 6; Charles Krupa/Photographer, p. 7; De Monstera Studio/Shutterstock.com, p. 8; © PolyPEDAL Lab UC Berkeley, p. 9; KenCanning/Getty Images p. 10; Courtesy of AeroVironment, Inc., pp. 11, 30; Uwe Bergwitz/Shutterstock.com, p. 12; © KIOST, p. 13; ANTON NAGY/Shutterstock.com, p. 14; Wyss Institute at Harvard University, p. 15; Shane Myers Photography/Shutterstock.com, p. 16; U.S. Navy photo by Mass Communication Specialist 3rd Class Edward Guttierrez III, p. 17; Andrew Atkinson/Shutterstock.com, p. 18; Julian Stratenschulte/dpa/Alamy Live News, p. 19; Thichaa/Shutterstock.com, pp. 20, 31; Professor Mark Cutkosky and Professor Sangbae Kim/MIT, p. 21; Independent birds/Shutterstock.com, p. 22; AP Photo/Imaginechina, p. 23; Feria Hikmet Noraddin/EyeEm/Getty Images, p. 24; AP Photo/Kai-Uwe Knoth, p. 25; Arisha Ray Singh/Shutterstock.com, p. 26; DOD Photo/Alamy Stock Photo, p. 27; David Havel/Shutterstock.com, p. 28; BAZA Production/Shutterstock.com, p. 29.

Cover images: Boston Globe/Getty Images; Franz Aberham/Getty Images; Bob_Eastman/iStock/Getty Images; Thierry Falise/LightRocket/Getty Images; Professor Mark Cutkosky and Professor Sangbae Kim/MIT.

Design elements: amgun/Getty Images; Mai Vu/Getty Images.